GW01326053

Original title:
Holding On to Us

Author: Kätriin Kaldaru
ISBN HARDBACK: 978-9916-89-793-5
ISBN PAPERBACK: 978-9916-89-794-2
ISBN EBOOK: 978-9916-89-795-9

Symphony of Souls United in Grace

In the stillness of the dawn, we rise,
Hearts entwined under the vast skies.
With a whisper of hope, we sing as one,
A melody of angels, our journey begun.

Grace surrounds us like a gentle breeze,
In each step of faith, our spirits seize.
Together we walk, hand in hand,
In the light of love, we firmly stand.

Through trials and storms, we find our way,
In sacred moments, we softly pray.
United in spirit, we've come to know,
The strength of our souls, in warmth they glow.

In every heartbeat, a promise anew,
Guided by faith, our vision is true.
With compassion abundant, we share our grace,
In this symphony blessed, we find our place.

As the stars align in the heavens above,
We dance to the rhythm of boundless love.
Together we flourish, our spirits aglow,
In this divine chorus, forever we'll flow.

Bonds Forged in Celestial Fire

In the forge of the stars we meet,
From ashes arise, our spirits greet.
United by faith, our hearts entwine,
In the luminous glow of divine design.

Each prayer a thread, each song a flame,
In celestial arms, we cast our name.
Together we soar, no fear, no strife,
In the sacred bond of eternal life.

Eternal Presence of Sacred Togetherness

In the stillness, where shadows blend,
A whisper of love, our hearts defend.
Hand in hand, we transcend the night,
In the sacred embrace of purest light.

Every moment a promise, every breath grace,
Together we journey, we find our place.
In laughter and tears, our spirits sing,
A hymn of togetherness, joy it brings.

The Heart's Guiding Light

In the depths of night, where darkness lays,
A spark ignites, our spirits blaze.
Guided by stars, we navigate true,
With love as our compass, we shall renew.

Each heartbeat a beacon, each sigh a prayer,
In the light of the heart, we lay ourselves bare.
Shining together, unwavering and bright,
We are one in the warmth of sacred light.

In the Refuge of Joined Spirits

In the sanctuary of souls combined,
Peace flows freely, wisdom defined.
We gather as one, in spirit we stand,
In the refuge of love, hand in hand.

Each story shared, a testament bold,
In the warmth of belonging, our faith unfolds.
Together we rise, shadows dispelled,
In the refuge of grace, forever upheld.

Cradle of Serenity Held by Love

In the arms of grace we lay,
Wrapped in light through night and day.
In whispers soft, our spirits soar,
Held by love forevermore.

In moments still, when silence speaks,
The heart finds peace, and hope it seeks.
A gentle touch, a warm embrace,
In love's cradle, we find our place.

Through trials faced and storms we brave,
In faith we stand, in love we save.
A bond unbroken, strong and true,
In this haven, I hold you.

When shadows fall and fears arise,
We rise as one, beneath the skies.
With every prayer and every sigh,
In love's embrace, we learn to fly.

In gratitude, our souls align,
With each heartbeat, your hand in mine.
In this cradle, we are blessed,
In love's journey, we find rest.

Tides of Faith and Togetherness

The tides of faith, they ebb and flow,
In unity, our spirits grow.
Through every wave, we stand as one,
In love's embrace, our hearts are spun.

As rivers merge and mountains stand,
Together, we will take our stand.
In storms we weather, through darkest night,
Our love shall be our guiding light.

In whispered dreams and silent prayers,
We journey forth, through trials and cares.
With hands entwined, we find our way,
In faith and love, we choose to stay.

Each step we take, a path we pave,
In every challenge, bold and brave.
Together we shall rise and sing,
In harmony, our spirits cling.

The ocean's song, a sacred tune,
In the dawn's light, beneath the moon.
Through tides of faith, forever blessed,
In bond of love, we find our rest.

Guiding Lights on Our Journey

The stars above, they gleam and glow,
Like guiding lights, their wisdom flows.
In darkest nights, they lead the way,
With faith our hearts shall not betray.

Each step we take, with courage found,
In love's embrace, we're heaven-bound.
Through trials faced, through joys we share,
Together, we rise, on wings of prayer.

In every heart, a flame ignites,
With love as our beacon, our spirits fight.
In shadows cast, we stand so tall,
With guiding lights, we shall not fall.

With open hearts, we walk this road,
In every burden, love will load.
With hands united, we face the storm,
In faith together, forever warm.

As dawn breaks clear, our voices sing,
In harmony, our praises ring.
For on this journey, hand in hand,
With guiding lights, together we stand.

In Unity, We Find Our Strength

In unity, our hearts align,
Bound by love, a thread divine.
Through trials faced, our spirits rise,
In every prayer, we touch the skies.

With open arms, we shelter all,
In love's embrace, we'll never fall.
Each joyful laugh, each tear we shed,
In unity, our hearts are fed.

Through darkest valleys, we will tread,
With faith as fuel and love ahead.
In every challenge that comes our way,
Together we stand, come what may.

In whispered dreams, our hopes take flight,
Through thick and thin, we'll find the light.
In every moment, strong and true,
In unity, I stand with you.

As seasons change and time moves on,
In love's embrace, we face the dawn.
Together forever, side by side,
In unity, our hearts abide.

When Hearts Align in Faith

In the stillness of the night,
We gather close in prayer,
Hearts entwined, spirits bright,
Guided by love's gentle care.

Each whisper shared in trust,
Strengthening our sacred vow,
In the ashes, rise we must,
With faith to lead us now.

Through trials that dim the light,
We stand firm, side by side,
With hope that shines so bright,
In God's embrace, we abide.

When shadows whisper doubts,
Together, we rise above,
In unity, we shout,
Our hearts pledge endless love.

With prayers woven like threads,
We build a fortress of grace,
Where every word that spreads,
Is a step in holy space.

A Lantern in the Darkness

In the depths of weary night,
A flicker appears divine,
Guiding souls with gentle light,
A beacon, forever mine.

When despair seeks to consume,
Your love shines ever bright,
In the cold, a flower blooms,
Illuminating the night.

With every prayer like a star,
We are drawn from dark to dawn,
Together, we wander far,
Believing hope is reborn.

In the silence of the space,
We find courage in the still,
As we seek His endless grace,
Our hearts forever will.

Hand in hand, we walk this way,
Each step lit by devotion,
In the night, we find our day,
A shared, unwavering ocean.

The Bond of Sacred Promises

With each vow, a light is born,
A bond formed by faith's embrace,
In the trials, we are sworn,
To hold love in every space.

Through the storms, we stand tall,
Unyielding in our sacred creed,
Together, we shall not fall,
For love is all we need.

Every promise, carved in stone,
A testament to our grace,
In this journey, never alone,
We thrive in faith's warm space.

With each tear that we share,
Our spirits deepen, align,
For in love we find our prayer,
A bond that stands the test of time.

In the light, our hearts entwined,
We rise above, hand in hand,
In this love, our souls aligned,
Forever, together we stand.

Guardian Light of Our Bond

In the gentle glow of dawn,
We find strength in sacred ties,
Each heartbeat, a vibrant song,
Echoing through endless skies.

As shadows darken the way,
We nurture the flame within,
With love, we shall not sway,
Our journey, where light begins.

The threads of faith, finely spun,
Weaves a tapestry of grace,
In this love, we are as one,
In its warmth, we find our place.

Every smile and every prayer,
Builds a bridge to the divine,
In the silence, we share,
Our hearts forever entwined.

Together, we shine so bright,
A testament to our bond,
Through the darkness, be our light,
Guardian love, forever fond.

With Every Breath, We Are One

In the silence of the night,
We whisper prayers to the divine.
Each heartbeat echoes in the light,
In unity, our spirits entwine.

Nature dances in sacred grace,
Creation sings in every breeze.
With every step, we find our place,
Connected in love that never flees.

The stars above our heads align,
Painting hope across the skies.
In every glance, a sacred sign,
Of love that never says goodbyes.

With each breath, a promise spares,
In thought and deed, we find our home.
We rise above our petty cares,
To the heavens, our spirits roam.

In the depth of our shared fight,
Hearts united, we stand tall.
In this journey, shining bright,
With every breath, we are one and all.

Divine Rays Illuminating Our Path

In the stillness of the dawn,
Holy rays break through the night.
Guiding souls that feel withdrawn,
Their warmth restores, their love ignites.

Each moment wrapped in grace,
Glimmers of hope, e'er illuminating.
With faith, we find our rightful place,
The path unfolds, invigorating.

Sunset paints the heavens gold,
The world bathed in tranquil hue.
In every story yet untold,
Divine whispers guide us through.

Waves of mercy crash ashore,
Carrying dreams, lost yet found.
With every heartbeat, we explore,
The sacred ground where love abounds.

In the embrace of divine light,
We tread upon this earthly canvas.
With open hearts, we rise in flight,
Illuminated, forever fabulous.

Angels Singing of Our Bonds

Hear the angels' sweet refrain,
Echoing love across the skies.
In their songs, we break our chains,
Harmony in their lullabies.

Voices meld in sacred union,
Uplifting hearts with every note.
In the dance of pure communion,
Together, we are destined to float.

As they weave the threads of fate,
Guiding us through joy and strife.
In every trial, they await,
To celebrate the gift of life.

Filling our hearts with peace profound,
Their watchful eyes, a soothing balm.
In faithful whispers, love abounds,
With every song, our spirits calm.

For in their presence, we are whole,
Bound together by threads unseen.
Angelic hymns that stir the soul,
In this tapestry, we glean.

Kinship in the Kingdom of Light

In the realm where shadows fade,
Unity graces every heart.
Hand in hand, we are remade,
A family formed, never to part.

Every smile, a sacred spark,
Bringing warmth to yearning souls.
Guided by love, we leave the dark,
Together we reach our noble goals.

Through trials faced, we learn to grow,
In this kingdom, we are blessed.
With compassion's light to bestow,
We find peace in each gentle quest.

In the laughter, joy takes flight,
Binding us in sacred trust.
Underneath the starry night,
In this kinship, only love is just.

Together we sing a timeless song,
In the harmony of shared grace.
In the kingdom, we all belong,
With every heart, we find our place.

Divine Ties Across the Cosmos

In the heavens' vast embrace,
Stars weave the tales of grace.
Celestial whispers softly flow,
Binding hearts, both high and low.

From distant realms, our spirits call,
Through sacred light, we stand tall.
In unity, our voices rise,
Echoes of love fill the skies.

The universe sings a hymn,
A melody pure, never dim.
In every soul, a spark divine,
Connecting threads that intertwine.

With each heartbeat, we proclaim,
The holy ties that bear His name.
Transcending time, in peace we roam,
Together we find our true home.

In faith's embrace, we are one,
Underneath the same bright sun.
As galaxies dance, we too unite,
In the sacred bond of the night.

When Hearts Commune in Grace

In the silence, whispers rise,
Hearts unite beneath the skies.
Grace flows gently, pure and sweet,
Guiding souls in love's heartbeat.

In humble prayer, our spirits soar,
Together we seek and implore.
Bound by hope, we stand in light,
Hand in hand, a wondrous sight.

Each shared moment blooms in faith,
A tapestry woven with grace.
In every tear, a story told,
The warmth of love, a shield we hold.

As sunlight breaks through darkest night,
Hearts entwined, embrace the light.
In every challenge, we shall find,
Communion of the heart and mind.

With each breath, we understand,
The sacred touch of God's own hand.
In unity, our spirits sing,
A symphony of hope we bring.

Light of Togetherness Shining Bright

In the twilight of our days,
Together we find countless ways.
To share the light, to spread the joy,
In every moment, we employ.

Hand in hand, we walk the path,
In love's embrace, escape the wrath.
As lanterns glow, our hearts ignite,
In every shadow, we find light.

The ties that bind are made of grace,
In each other's smiles, we find our place.
Through trials faced and joys achieved,
Together in faith, we are relieved.

With every dawn, new hope we see,
In togetherness, we shall be free.
The radiance of love's pure fire,
Ignites our souls, lifts us higher.

As stars align in the darkest night,
We stand as one, hearts burning bright.
In the warmth of love's embrace,
Together we journey, full of grace.

The Covenant of Our Spirits

In sacred stillness, pledges made,
A covenant of hearts displayed.
With whispered vows, we intertwine,
In faith and love, our lives align.

From depths of sorrow, joy will rise,
A promise sealed beneath the skies.
Through trials faced, we hold the line,
In every struggle, love will shine.

The threads of life, both strong and frail,
We weave as one, to never fail.
In every bond, a story's told,
Of courage found, of hearts consoled.

As seasons change, we stand steadfast,
United in love, a bond to last.
In every heartbeat, grace flows free,
A covenant forged in harmony.

In sacred moments, we shall pray,
Our spirits lift, come what may.
Together we rise, like the sun's embrace,
In the dance of faith, we find our place.

Everlasting Grace Between Us

In the whispers of dawn's light,
We find grace woven tight.
Hands clasped in sacred trust,
Hearts aligned, pure and just.

In trials we seek His face,
Guided by everlasting grace.
Each step, a holy dance,
A love born of chance.

Through storms we remain whole,
Bound by a single soul.
Faith anchors us deep,
Promises we always keep.

With every breath we take,
In His arms, we awake.
In joy and peace, we blend,
Together till the end.

Sanctuary of Silent Prayers

In shadows where stillness breathes,
A sanctuary, the soul receives.
Whispers of love, softly spoken,
A bond unbreakable, never broken.

The heart, an altar pure,
In silence, we find our cure.
Gratitude fills the space,
In every challenge, His grace.

Upon the walls, hope resides,
In shadows, our faith abides.
Each tear, a prayer's release,
In the quiet, we find peace.

Together we rise and fall,
In stillness, we hear His call.
Our spirits soar, forever connected,
In silent prayers, re-directed.

Mirrored Souls in Reverence

In the depths of shared reflection,
Two souls dance in connection.
Mirrored glances, a sacred trust,
United as one, we must.

With every trial, we stand tall,
In faith, we rise, we do not fall.
Bound by love, forever entwined,
In sacred moments, we find.

Every heartbeat, a chance to pray,
In reverence, we find our way.
Through trials, joy will bloom,
In our hearts, there is room.

With hands held in grace,
We journey through every space.
Mirrored souls, a holy blend,
In love, we begin and end.

Reflections in Divine Love

In every sunrise, whispers sound,
Divine love, profoundly found.
Hearts uplifted, spirits soar,
In His embrace, forevermore.

In the quiet, truths unfold,
Stories of grace, lovingly told.
Mirroring the heavens above,
We walk in the light of love.

Every moment, a sacred gift,
In our hearts, His spirit lifts.
Through reflections, we see the way,
Guided by love, day by day.

With each step on this path we share,
In divine love, we boldly dare.
Together we shine, forever bright,
In the warmth of His light.

The Sanctuary of Our Union

In quiet corners, two hearts meet,
Beneath the gaze of stars so bright,
In whispered prayers, our souls entwine,
Bound by faith, a sacred light.

Hand in hand, we walk the path,
Through trials fierce, our spirits soar,
With every step, we find our grace,
In love's embrace, forevermore.

The world may tempt with shadows deep,
Yet here we stand, steadfast and true,
In this sanctuary, hope does bloom,
Together forged, our bond anew.

With every tear, a lesson learned,
In joy and sorrow, we find our way,
In unity, we seek the divine,
Guided by love, come what may.

So let this union shine so bright,
A beacon in the night's long breath,
In each other's arms, we find our peace,
A promise kept, defying death.

Hands Clasped in Devotion

Hands clasped tight in fervent prayer,
Voices rise like morning dew,
In the silence, we draw near,
Hearts ablaze with love so true.

Together we seek the sacred truth,
In the whispers of ancient ways,
United by faith, we stand as one,
Divine light guiding all our days.

In humble acts, our spirits soar,
With every kindness, we embrace,
The light of grace, our guiding star,
In service given, we find our place.

So let our hands forever join,
In every trial, we find our strength,
With love as deep as oceans wide,
Together walking any length.

In devotion's arms, we hold each other,
At the altar of our dreams we kneel,
In faith, we rise and never falter,
Bound eternally in love we feel.

Remnants of Belief

In the echoes of ancient songs,
Resides the whispers of our past,
We gather here, where hope begun,
In remnants of belief, we are cast.

Through the storms, we seek the light,
With every struggle, our spirits grow,
In shadows deep, we find our faith,
A flicker strong, its warmth we know.

So many doubts may cloud our way,
Yet in our hearts, the truth remains,
In every trial, love's gentle grace,
Transforms our pain into holy grains.

Among the broken, we find our strength,
In every tear, a seed of peace,
Together we rise with each new dawn,
In every challenge, we find release.

These remnants of belief we hold,
With open hearts, we journey through,
In the silent places, hope ignites,
And fills our lives with light anew.

The Word Made Flesh in Us

In humble forms, His love appears,
Through gentle smiles and whispered grace,
The Word made flesh, our hearts embrace,
With every moment, we draw near.

In acts of love, His spirit flows,
Through hands that heal and voices strong,
In kindness shared, His truth it shows,
Together, we create a song.

In sacred spaces, shadows flee,
As light emerges, bright and pure,
In every heartbeat, He is we,
In faith's embrace, our souls endure.

The Word made flesh, alive in sight,
Through trials faced, we find our way,
With open hearts, we chase the light,
With every breath, our spirits sway.

So let us share this holy gift,
To bear His love in all we do,
Together risen, hearts adrift,
In unity, we find what's true.

A Tapestry of Prayer and Presence

In the stillness we gather, seeking grace,
Threads of devotion woven in space.
Hearts whisper softly, hands raised high,
In unity we lift our prayers to the sky.

With each breath, the spirit ignites,
In sacred silence, our souls take flight.
Bonded by faith, we walk as one,
A tapestry of light beneath the sun.

Through trials and joys, we stand as kin,
The fabric of prayer wraps us within.
Voices uplifted, the chorus is strong,
Together we find where we all belong.

In moments of doubt, we find our way,
Guided by love, come what may.
Every prayer a stitch, every moment a thread,
In this sacred dance, our hearts are fed.

As dusk falls gently, we gather close,
Embracing the quiet, we feel the most.
In the warmth of togetherness, we reside,
In a tapestry of love, forever tied.

Together Under the Gaze of the Divine

Beneath the heavens, our spirits entwine,
In the glow of faith, together we shine.
Each soul a star, bright and unique,
United in purpose, together we seek.

With hands clasped gently, we bow our heads,
In the quiet moment, where our heart leads.
The divine gaze watching, a love so near,
In the sanctuary of prayer, we find our cheer.

Voices rise softly, a meditative sound,
In the embrace of the sacred, hope is found.
Together we journey, through light and dark,
Guided by grace, igniting a spark.

Every heartbeat echoes in perfect time,
The rhythm of faith, a celestial chime.
Together we stand, facing the dawn,
Under the gaze of the divine, we go on.

In community strong, we share our grace,
Bound by the love that time won't erase.
Together we flourish, together we soar,
Under the gaze of the divine, forevermore.

Symphony of Hearts in Reverence

In the gathering light, our spirits align,
A symphony of hearts, together divine.
With every whisper, a note takes flight,
In reverence we stand, through the day and night.

Chords of compassion, we weave with care,
In harmony's grace, we learn to share.
Each soul a melody, rich and bright,
Together we sing, finding strength in the light.

With faith as our guide, we rise and embrace,
In the sacred dance, we find our place.
Resounding in love, our voices soar,
In a symphony of hearts, we are forevermore.

Together we journey, through valleys and peaks,
The music of hope, in silence it speaks.
Each heartbeat a rhythm, a prayer in the still,
In trust we unite, surrendering our will.

As the echoes linger, in the twilight's glow,
We cherish the bond that continues to grow.
A symphony of hearts, with grace we convene,
In reverence we find where we have been.

In the Shadow of Sacred Pines

In the shadows deep where the pines stand tall,
We find a sanctuary, a holy call.
Leaves whisper secrets, the earth breathes slow,
In stillness we gather, our spirits aglow.

Each prayer a seed, planted with care,
In the soil of faith, we bloom and share.
Nature surrounds us, a chorus of grace,
In the shadow of pines, we find our place.

With every petal that falls to the ground,
The circle of life, in silence profound.
Here in the woods, where the spirit flows,
In the shadow of pines, our love only grows.

We share our stories, our hopes intertwined,
Each voice a blessing, in unison aligned.
Together we breathe, under sacred skies,
In the shadow of pines, our souls arise.

As the sun dips low, painting the night,
With hearts full of wonder, we embrace the light.
In communion we stand, a tranquil sign,
Forever we flourish, in the shadow of pines.

Resilience Beneath the Veil of Time

In the quiet whispers of the night,
Faith blooms softly, holding tight.
Each moment, a chance to rise,
With hope that never fades or dies.

The storms may come, the shadows cast,
Yet courage shines, forever steadfast.
Through every trial, we find our way,
Resilience blooms in the light of day.

The sands of time may shift and sway,
But hearts grow stronger, come what may.
Beneath the veil, a light does shine,
In every soul, a love divine.

In silence, prayers weave through the air,
Infusing strength with gentle care.
Through pain and joy, we rise and bend,
Our spirits lifted, hearts will mend.

So trust the path that lies ahead,
With faith as guide, we won't dread.
Together we stand, one hand in hand,
In resilience, united, we shall stand.

Threads of Grace in Every Breath

In every breath, a whisper sweet,
Grace entwined in life's heartbeat.
With each sunrise, blessings fall,
Threads of love, binding us all.

The gentle breeze holds secrets dear,
Carrying hope, casting out fear.
In quiet moments, we receive,
Faith's soft voice, teaching to believe.

The tapestry of life unfolds,
In faded dreams, and stories told.
Knots of trial, seams of peace,
In grace, our burdens find release.

United, hearts like rivers flow,
Through valleys deep, and fields aglow.
Each thread is woven, pure and true,
In every life, a sacred view.

So breathe in deeply, trust the grace,
Find strength in love's warm embrace.
For threads of truth will always bind,
In every soul, the divine designed.

Navigating Life with Sacred Hands

With sacred hands, we journey forth,
Drawn by love, ignited by worth.
In every act, a prayer we weave,
Guiding souls, together we believe.

The path may twist, and turns may bring,
But hearts aligned will always sing.
Through shadows dark, we hold the light,
With sacred hands, dispelling night.

In laughter shared and tears released,
We find our strength, our souls at peace.
Through every challenge, we expand,
With faith as compass, guided and planned.

So let us walk with purpose true,
In every moment, something new.
With sacred hands, we tend the flame,
In love and service, we share the name.

Together we'll navigate the storm,
With sacred hands, we create the warm.
In unity, our hearts will soar,
In every breath, we seek to restore.

The Blessing of Shared Paths

In every stride, a blessing found,
Walking together on holy ground.
With hearts aligned, we share the way,
In love's embrace, we choose to stay.

Through winding roads and open skies,
In every glance, a sacred prize.
As whispers guide, we journey on,
In trust unbroken, fears are gone.

The blessings flow like rivers wide,
In shared laughter, side by side.
Through laughter's light and sorrow's tears,
We share the weight, ease all our fears.

With each shared step, the bond grows strong,
In every moment, we belong.
In the tapestry of life we weave,
Together we rise, together we believe.

So let's embrace this sacred choice,
In harmony, we lift our voice.
The blessing of paths, hand in hand,
Together in love, forever we stand.

Beneath the Wings of Angels

In shadows deep, their presence glows,
Guardians wise, in love they flow.
With whispers soft, they guide our way,
In darkened hours, they bring the day.

Their wings enfold, a gentle shield,
With faith and hope, our hearts are healed.
In every prayer, their light appears,
To calm the storm, to dry our tears.

When doubt clouds the path we tread,
Angels lift us, where fear has bled.
Their songs of grace, like morning dew,
Quench the soul, and make it new.

Beneath their wings, we find our peace,
In sacred love, our fears decrease.
With spirits bright, they lift our gaze,
In unity, we sing their praise.

Threads of Eternity We Weave

In every heart, a thread of gold,
Woven tight, yet free and bold.
We stitch our dreams with love and care,
A tapestry, all souls laid bare.

Through laughter warm, and sorrow's tear,
Each strand of life, draws us near.
Intertwined, in joy and strife,
We find the sacred dance of life.

With every act, the fabric grows,
In kindness sown, true beauty shows.
Respites taken, hope bestowed,
In every heart, the love has flowed.

Threads of grace, in colors bright,
Guide us through the darkest night.
Together bound, our spirits twine,
In harmony, our souls align.

Echoes of Heaven's Affection

In every dawn, the light is born,
A promise kept through night and scorn.
Each breeze that flows is sent from grace,
A whisper soft, in every place.

Within the heart, the echoes sing,
Of love profound, our offering.
With each embrace, the world reflects,
The sacred bond that faith connects.

Through valleys deep, and mountains high,
The heart of heaven cannot lie.
In peace profound, our spirits soar,
To realms of love, and evermore.

In quiet moments, truth revealed,
In every sorrow, joy is healed.
We find our strength, in love's pure light,
Guided by faith, through darkest night.

The Sacred Circle of Kinship

In sacred bonds, we gather near,
A circle strong, in love sincere.
With open hearts, we share our grace,
Embracing all, in this holy place.

Together we stand, as one in prayer,
In every joy, in every care.
In laughter shared, our spirits rise,
Reflecting love beneath the skies.

Through trials faced, we bear the load,
In kinship's warmth, we find our road.
With hands entwined, we journey on,
In faith united, we are strong.

Each story told, a thread divine,
In every heart, a legacy shines.
Around this circle, we find our way,
In love eternal, we choose to stay.

Bonds Beyond the Veil

In shadows cast by fleeting time,
We hold a love that feels divine.
A tether strong that will not break,
In every breath, our hopes awake.

Though earthly ties may fade and wane,
Our spirits dance through joy and pain.
In sacred realms, our hearts entwine,
Beyond the veil, your soul is mine.

Through trials faced, we stand as one,
A journey shared, yet just begun.
With faith as our unyielding guide,
Together still, we'll always stride.

In whispered prayers, we find our way,
In light and love that will not sway.
This bond we share, a holy flame,
In every heartbeat, call my name.

When time shall cease and shadows flee,
Our eternal love shall ever be.
In realms unknown, we shall reside,
Bonds beyond the veil, our hearts abide.

Eternal Whispers of Love

In tranquil nights, the stars align,
Your voice, a melody divine.
Each whisper carries sacred grace,
A love that time cannot erase.

Among the clouds, our spirits soar,
In every heartbeat, we explore.
The gentle breeze sings soft and low,
A hymn of love that ever grows.

Through trials faced and rivers crossed,
In faith, we find what once was lost.
Together, hand in hand we strive,
With love eternal, we will thrive.

In every shadow, light we find,
Our souls entwined, forever kind.
These whispered vows, our sacred thread,
In love's embrace, we'll never dread.

Across the ages, we shall weave,
A tapestry of love, believe.
In every breath, a promise shared,
Eternal whispers, always bared.

Souls in Sacred Harmony

In sacred space where silence reigns,
Our spirits dance, breaking the chains.
With every note, our hearts align,
In harmony, your soul is mine.

The sacred song of love we sing,
In joyful praise, our praises ring.
Through trials faced, we find the way,
To light the dark, to greet the day.

With every challenge, hand in hand,
In faith and trust, together stand.
Our souls entwined, like roots of trees,
In sacred harmony, we find ease.

In moments shared, our spirits rise,
Reflections of celestial skies.
With every heartbeat, stronger still,
In love's embrace, we bend our will.

Forever bound, we walk this path,
In sacred spaces, share our wrath.
This journey blessed by love above,
Souls in sacred harmony, our love.

Anchored in Grace

In storms of life, where tempests roar,
We find our peace on grace's shore.
With faith as our unyielding sail,
Anchored in love, we shall not fail.

Through trials faced and shadows cast,
Our hearts entwined, forever steadfast.
In every moment rich with grace,
Together still, we'll find our place.

With every heartbeat, calm resides,
In gentle whispers, love abides.
With gratitude that we embrace,
Each precious gift, a warm embrace.

In quietude, the spirit sings,
A song of hope, of blessed things.
Through every burden, we shall find,
Anchored in grace, our hearts aligned.

As seasons change and years go by,
With faith in heart, we touch the sky.
In love's embrace, we'll always trace,
Our journey blessed, anchored in grace.

The Sacred Choir of Togetherness

In harmony we rise and sing,
Voices blend, our spirits cling.
With faith's light, we find our way,
Together, brightening the day.

Hand in hand, we form a chain,
Through joy and sorrow, love remains.
In every heart, a spark ignites,
Guiding each soul to the heights.

With every prayer, we weave our fate,
In unity, we celebrate.
The sacred bond, a treasure sweet,
In every challenge, we find our beat.

Let kindness flow, a river wide,
In love's embrace, we shall abide.
With open hearts, we share the grace,
As one, we seek the holy space.

Together we shall walk the path,
In light and laughter, love's aftermath.
The sacred choir, a melody true,
In every note, we are renewed.

Celestial Paths to One Another

Beneath the stars, our spirits meet,
In whispers soft, our hearts repeat.
The universe draws us near,
Finding grace in every tear.

As moonlight dances on the stream,
We walk in faith, a shared dream.
With every step, a promise made,
A bond of love that will not fade.

Through valleys low and mountains high,
We soar together, ever nigh.
In silence heard, in laughter spilled,
With every breath, our souls are filled.

The road is long, but hand in hand,
We trace the path, together we stand.
The light of hope forever shines,
In every heart, a love that binds.

As celestial sparks guide our way,
We gather strength in the light of day.
In paths aligned, we find our grace,
United in this sacred space.

Eternal Embrace of the Divine

In the stillness, silence speaks,
The divine presence ever seeks.
With each heartbeat, love flows free,
An eternal bond, you and me.

In moments shared, we feel the grace,
The sacred touch, a warm embrace.
Through trials faced, we grow so strong,
In every note, we sing our song.

The breath of life within us stirs,
In gentle whispers, the spirit purrs.
Every soul, a sacred spark,
Illuminating the deepest dark.

In love's embrace, we find our home,
No longer lost, no more to roam.
Divine connection, vast and grand,
Together we walk, hand in hand.

In every heartbeat, love is born,
With open arms, we greet the morn.
The divine dance, a radiant flow,
In eternal love, we grow.

Sacred Threads of Togetherness

In the tapestry of life we weave,
Each thread a story, we believe.
With golden ties, our hearts align,
In every moment, love divine.

From every hue, a bond is cast,
Together, we embrace the vast.
Through laughter shared and tears we shed,
In sacred threads, our spirits led.

With gentle hands, we mend the seams,
In unity, we foster dreams.
Through storms and sunlight, side by side,
In every challenge, love abides.

The woven fabric, strong and bright,
A testament to our shared light.
In every stitch, a tale unfolds,
Of love profound and hope that holds.

Together stitched, we stand as one,
In every dawn, a new day's sun.
The sacred threads, forever true,
In this great circle, me and you.

When Hearts Align with Grace

In the stillness of the night,
Hearts whisper to the stars,
Bound by threads of purest light,
Embraced in love from afar.

In unity, we stand as one,
Guided by a gentle hand,
Through the shadows, we will run,
Together, a sacred band.

With each step, faith interweaves,
A melody soft and true,
In the tapestry of leaves,
We find purpose in our view.

In the silence, echoes ring,
Of kindness woven in grace,
Hope and love in the wind sing,
As hearts align in this space.

So let us gather, hand in hand,
With a vision bright and clear,
In God's garden, we will stand,
Fostering love year by year.

In the Heart of the Divine Embrace

Within the heart where spirit flows,
A sanctuary of peace,
In the depths of love's repose,
All burdens find their release.

Here in silence, whispers rise,
Carried on the gentle breeze,
The wisdom of the skies,
Brings comfort to our knees.

In every prayer, in every song,
The bonds of faith unite,
With every moment, we belong,
In the sacred morning light.

Like branches reaching toward the sun,
We stretch in love's pure grace,
In the heart of everyone,
We find our rightful place.

Together in this sacred space,
We forge a path untold,
In the heart of divine embrace,
Love's story will unfold.

The Flame of Our Collective Essence

From the depths of every soul,
A flame ignites, fierce and bright,
Together, we are made whole,
Guided by a sacred light.

In the gathering of our dreams,
A warmth begins to rise,
Unity flows in gentle streams,
Connecting hearts and skies.

With each flicker, each small spark,
We illuminate the night,
In the silence, we embark,
To share the love and light.

Through trials and through pain,
Our essence shines like gold,
In the joy, we seek to gain,
Our stories will be told.

So let this flame forever blaze,
In every heart it's found,
Together, we will always raise,
Our voices in the sound.

Shared Sacred Dreams Under Heaven

In the twilight, hopes awake,
We gather 'neath the stars,
In the stillness, love's a lake,
Reflecting who we are.

With every dream, we weave a thread,
A tapestry of grace,
Stories shared, seeds we spread,
In this sacred place.

Through every tear, through every laugh,
We nurture what we find,
Navigating life's long path,
Together, intertwined.

Underneath the vast expanse,
We find solace in the night,
In the rhythm, we will dance,
As spirits take their flight.

So let us cherish every dream,
In the light of heaven's glow,
With love as our constant theme,
Together, we will grow.

In the Sanctuary of Our Souls

Within the heart, a sacred place,
Where light and grace find their embrace.
Each whispered prayer, a gentle sigh,
Invoking love that can't deny.

In quiet halls where spirits dwell,
We listen close to every bell.
The echoes of the soul's deep call,
Remind us we are one and all.

Beneath the stars, in stillness found,
Our hopes ascend, the ties profound.
In every tear and joyful song,
A tapestry where we belong.

Through trials faced and burdens borne,
In unity, our hearts reborn.
For in the dark, the light breaks through,
Guiding us to what is true.

So let us dwell within this space,
A haven filled with love and grace.
In the sanctuary of our souls,
Together, we shall reach our goals.

Anchored in Celestial Love

When storms arise and shadows fall,
We find our strength in love's great call.
With every breath, we hold it near,
A promise whispered, crystal clear.

The stars above, like eyes that see,
Illuminate the path to be.
In every heart, a shining light,
Guiding us through the darkest night.

Anchored firm, our souls will soar,
With faith as vast as ocean floor.
In love's embrace, we stand as one,
United beneath the setting sun.

For in the heights of boundless grace,
We seek the truth in every place.
Celestial songs upon the breeze,
Remind us all to kneel and please.

Through valleys low and mountains high,
Our spirits rise, we learn to fly.
Anchored in love, we shall remain,
Embracing hope through joy and pain.

Cherished Bonds of Faith

A circle strong, our hands entwined,
In shared belief, our hearts aligned.
Through trials faced and journeys made,
In love's sweet light, we are displayed.

Each story told, a lesson learned,
In every soul, a fire burned.
Together we walk on sacred ground,
Where cherished bonds of faith abound.

In laughter shared and tears released,
We find our solace and our peace.
With every prayer, we lift the veil,
And weave the threads of love's own tale.

Through darkened nights and brighter days,
We shine our light in countless ways.
In faith's embrace, we stand secure,
With hearts attuned, our spirits pure.

So let us gather, side by side,
In cherished bonds, we will abide.
With hope renewed, we shall aspire,
To walk together, hearts on fire.

Whispered Prayers in Unity

In stillness deep, our voices rise,
Like morning mist beneath the skies.
Whispered prayers, a bridge we weave,
In unity, we shall believe.

Each fervent word, a sacred plea,
A calling forth what's yet to be.
With hands uplifted, we embrace,
The gift of love, of boundless grace.

In hearts aligned, we find our strength,
Together we go to any length.
Through whispered prayers, our spirits soar,
An anthem sung forevermore.

As seasons change and time moves on,
In unity, we will be strong.
For in each echo, faith ignites,
A flame of hope that ever lights.

So let our prayers like rivers flow,
In whispered love, together grow.
In every soul, a sacred part,
In unity, we share one heart.

Finding Home in Each Other's Eyes

In the warmth of your gaze, I see my soul,
Whispers of grace that make me whole.
In silence, our hearts, a sacred space,
Finding home in love, in each embrace.

Through trials we walk, hand in hand,
Together we rise, together we stand.
In storms of doubt, I find my peace,
In your eyes, the chaos will cease.

With every tear, our joys entwine,
Strengthened by faith, our spirits shine.
In laughter and prayer, our voices soar,
Finding home in truth, forevermore.

Your laughter a beacon, your smile a light,
Guiding my heart through the darkest night.
In the tapestry of life, we are sewn,
Finding home in love, we are never alone.

With each gentle word and tender sigh,
I am anchored by love that cannot die.
In the embrace of your truth divine,
Finding home in each other's eyes, so fine.

The Gift of Togetherness in Prayer

Hand in hand, we seek the skies,
Voices lifted, our spirits rise.
In humble praise, our hearts unite,
The gift of togetherness, our light.

In moments of quiet, we find our way,
With open hearts, we long to stay.
Each whispered prayer, a gentle grace,
A sacred bond in this holy space.

Through trials and joys, we stand as one,
In the love of our faith, battles are won.
In every tear, in every cheer,
The gift of togetherness, ever near.

All burdens shared, a weightless load,
With faith as our guide, we walk the road.
In gratitude's glow, we find our beat,
The gift of togetherness makes us complete.

Together we rise, together we fall,
In the warmth of His love, we hear the call.
In every moment, united we pray,
The gift of togetherness lights the way.

Echoes of Love, Forever Echoing

In the chambers of our hearts, love sings,
Echoes of joy, the light it brings.
With every heartbeat, our spirits soar,
Echoes of love, forevermore.

In the stillness of night, whispers flow,
Soft as the stars that gently glow.
Through trials faced, and tears we shed,
Echoes of love, where hope is fed.

The beauty of grace, in moments shared,
Guiding our path when life seems bare.
In the dance of time, in sacred space,
Echoes of love, the sweetest grace.

In the tapestry woven by hands divine,
Every thread a promise, forever entwined.
In laughter and sorrow, we rise above,
Echoes of love, binding us like a glove.

With every prayer and kind embrace,
We find our journey, a holy race.
In the chorus of life, we hear the call,
Echoes of love, forever echoing all.

Strong Roots in the Garden of Faith

In the soil of trust, our roots run deep,
Nurtured by love, a promise we keep.
Through storms we bend, yet never break,
Strong roots in faith, a love to make.

In sunlight's warmth, we find our peace,
The garden of grace brings sweet release.
With every bloom, our spirits thrive,
Strong roots in faith, together we strive.

In seasons of doubt, we hold on tight,
With prayer as our compass, we find our light.
In fellowship's shade, we gather round,
Strong roots in faith, where hope is found.

As branches reach high, we share the dream,
In the garden of life, we are a team.
Through trials faced, we rise above,
Strong roots in faith, watered by love.

With hearts aligned, we cultivate grace,
In the garden of faith, we find our place.
In every prayer, in every sigh,
Strong roots in the garden, we will not die.

Unity in the Embrace of Grace

In shadows cast by fervent light,
We gather close, a bond so tight.
In silent prayer, hearts entwined,
Each soul a mirror, love defined.

With hands uplifted to the skies,
We find our strength; the spirit flies.
In harmony, our voices rise,
A chorus sung, where divinity lies.

Through trials faced, we rise anew,
In faith we walk, our path is true.
With every step, grace guides our way,
In unity, we choose to stay.

The world may tremble, storms may bend,
Yet in this love, we shall transcend.
With hearts aflame, our hopes embrace,
In every moment, find His grace.

Together we stand, side by side,
In love's embrace, we will abide.
With gentle hands, we lift and pray,
In God's sweet light, we find our way.

Celestial Encounters in Stillness

In the hush of night, we softly gaze,
Upon the stars, in heaven's blaze.
With whispered dreams, our spirits soar,
In stillness found, we seek for more.

The moon bestows its silver light,
Guiding hearts through the sacred night.
In quietude, the soul's response,
A dance of faith, the stars ensconce.

Through sacred silence, wisdom speaks,
In every pause, the heart then seeks.
To hear the truths that softly call,
In moments still, we feel it all.

With every breath, we find release,
In cosmic love, we seek our peace.
The universe sings, so vast, so bright,
In celestial realms, we find our light.

Together we wander, hand in hand,
In unity, forever we stand.
The stars align, in sweet embrace,
In every heartbeat, know His grace.

Interwoven Souls Beneath the Stars

Beneath the arch of timeless night,
Our souls entwined, in shared delight.
With every glance, a story told,
In cosmic threads of love, we hold.

In whispered winds, our secrets share,
A tapestry woven with tender care.
As constellations guide our way,
With faith as bright as break of day.

In silence, we find a sacred space,
Where every heartbeat echoes grace.
With open hearts, we dare to dream,
In unity deep, we are redeemed.

Through trials faced, we rise as one,
With every dawn, a new day begun.
In harmony, our spirits sing,
In love's embrace, we find our wings.

With every star that lights the night,
We are connected in His sight.
Interwoven souls, forever free,
In sacred bonds, we are, we be.

Love's Sacred Pilgrimage

With weary footsteps, we walk this road,
Through valleys deep, our hearts bestowed.
In love's pure light, we find our way,
A sacred journey, come what may.

Each mile we trod, with faith ablaze,
In trials faced, we lift our praise.
The path may twist, yet hope will gleam,
In every heartbeat, chase the dream.

Through sunlit days and stormy skies,
We see the truth in each other's eyes.
In love's embrace, a guiding hand,
Together we journey, together we stand.

As every tear gives birth to grace,
We rise anew, in love's embrace.
With courage found in shared despair,
On this pilgrimage, our spirits share.

With every step, our bond ignites,
In love's great warmth, we find our rights.
In sacred moments, hearts align,
Together forever, your hand in mine.

Celestial Threads of Destiny

In the tapestry of stars, we weave,
The dreams that guide us, we believe.
Each thread a story, intertwined,
In heavenly realms, our fates aligned.

With purpose bright, the paths unfold,
A cosmic dance, the tales retold.
In every heartbeat lies the grace,
Of destinies in time and space.

Through trials faced, and shadows cast,
We find the light, our hearts steadfast.
The universe speaks, a gentle sign,
In every moment, love will shine.

Together we walk, hand in hand,
In sacred trust, together we stand.
The stars above, our witnesses true,
In celestial threads, I find you.

Forever bound by love's embrace,
In the journey of life, we find our place.
Eternal echoes of the soul's song,
In destiny's weave, we both belong.

Embracing the Divine in Each Other

Within your gaze, a light so bright,
A mirror holding the purest light.
In your embrace, I feel the grace,
Of love divine, our sacred space.

Hearts entwined, we rise and fall,
In unity, we heed the call.
With every prayer, a whispered vow,
We honor the gift of our love now.

Through trials faced, with faith we tread,
In each heartbeat, the spirit's spread.
Together we nurture this holy flame,
In love's embrace, we share a name.

With open hearts, we share our dreams,
In every moment, the spirit gleams.
Embracing the divine, we find our way,
In love's embrace, forever we stay.

In sacred moments, we find our truth,
Each breath a blessing, the joy of youth.
Together we stand, through joy and strife,
Embracing the divine, the dance of life.

Soulful Whispers on the Wind

The wind carries whispers, soft and clear,
Echoes of love, for only you to hear.
In every breeze, a gentle sigh,
The language of souls, as they fly high.

Through the trees, secrets softly flow,
In nature's heart, our spirits grow.
The rustling leaves, a choir of grace,
In the sacred space, we find our place.

Moments of silence, a knowing glance,
In nature's rhythm, we join the dance.
The world around us, alive with sound,
In soulful whispers, our truths are found.

As daylight fades, and stars ignite,
Our souls entwined in the starry night.
In tranquil thoughts, we drift and blend,
In whispers of love, we ascend.

With each caress, the universe sings,
The joy in our hearts, and the hope it brings.
Through whispers on the wind, we soar,
In love's embrace, forever more.

The Blessed Union of the Heart

In sacred vows, our hearts shall bind,
A union blessed, a love defined.
Through trials faced, our spirits soar,
In harmony, we seek to explore.

With every glance, the promise made,
In love's embrace, our fears allayed.
Together we dream, with faith so strong,
In this blessed union, we belong.

Through storms and sun, we stand as one,
In laughter's glow, our lives begun.
With gentle touch, and kindness sown,
In love's embrace, we are not alone.

The journey forward, hand in hand,
The light of hope, a guiding strand.
In every heartbeat, a love that's true,
In this blessed union, just me and you.

As time unfolds, our story grows,
In every chapter, love continuously flows.
In the tapestry of life, forever part,
In the blessed union of the heart.

Graceful Journeys Hand in Hand

With faith as our guide, we walk the path,
Through valleys of doubt, through moments of wrath.
In harmony, we share each step we take,
A bond of belief, in the love we make.

Through storms that may come, our spirits stay bright,
In whispers of hope, we find our true light.
Together we rise, like the sun in the morn,
In the grace of His presence, anew we are born.

With prayers in our hearts, our voices ascend,
In unity's shelter, our souls will depend.
Hand in hand, we wander, through trials and grace,
Each journey we take, His love we embrace.

In laughter and tears, we'll carry our dreams,
As rivers of faith flow in joined streams.
With each passing moment, our spirits entwine,
Each journey we cherish, forever divine.

Unbroken Chains of Belief

In times of despair, our hearts remain bold,
For faith is the treasure that never grows old.
With hands clasped in prayer, we gather in grace,
In unbroken chains, we find our true place.

Through shadows of doubt, our spirits will rise,
Together we see the light in the skies.
With visions of love, we mend every tear,
In the bonds of our faith, we find strength to share.

Each promise we make, a beacon of hope,
Through trials and storms, together we cope.
In the whispers of truth, our hearts will be free,
Unbroken by time, forever we'll be.

With souls intertwined, the journey is bright,
Our belief is the compass that leads us to light.
As long as we stand, with courage and grace,
In the unbroken chains, we find our true place.

In the Garden of Our Hearts

In the garden of souls, where love blossoms fair,
Each moment we nurture, with tenderest care.
Through seasons of change, together we grow,
In faith's gentle breeze, our spirits will glow.

The flowers of kindness, we plant and we sow,
With prayers as the sun, our hearts overflow.
In the depth of our vows, we reap what we share,
In the garden of hearts, His love is our prayer.

With roots intertwined, we weather the storms,
In unity's grace, our true selves transform.
As petals of joy spread their fragrance divine,
In the garden of hope, our spirits align.

Each moment we tend, in laughter, in tears,
Through the seasons of life, we conquer our fears.
In the garden of faith, we find our new start,
With love as our harvest, we cultivate heart.

The Light We Share Above

In the stillness of night, a star shines so bright,
A beacon of hope, our guiding light.
With hearts open wide, we gaze at the sky,
The light that we share, a spark that won't die.

Through trials we face, its warmth keeps us whole,
In whispers of faith, we comfort the soul.
With love as our anchor, we reach for the stars,
In the light we share, we heal all our scars.

Together we shine, a tapestry bold,
In countless reflections, our stories unfold.
With hands raised in praise, we dance in His grace,
For the light that we share, a sacred embrace.

In moments of silence, in laughter, in song,
The light we believe in, forever stays strong.
With joy in our hearts, and faith as our guide,
The light we share above, forever our pride.

Cherished Moments in the Heart's Canvas

In sacred stillness, moments shared,
Each glance a prayer, tenderly bared.
With faith as our guide, love gently flows,
In the heart's canvas, beauty grows.

From laughter to tears, a divine embrace,
In every heartbeat, we find our place.
Together we wander, hand in hand,
In the light of grace, forever we stand.

Eternal whispers echo in time,
Marking each heartbeat, a sacred rhyme.
In cherished moments, His spirit ignites,
Lighting our path through the darkest nights.

Through struggles and trials, love is our shield,
In faith's gentle arms, our wounds are healed.
With hope as our anchor, we rise and soar,
In the heart's canvas, we seek evermore.

Each stroke of kindness, a blessing bestowed,
In shared laughter, our joys overflowed.
With love as our compass, we navigate life,
In cherished moments, we conquer the strife.

The Beatitudes of Togetherness

Blessed are those who gather in peace,
In unity found, their spirits release.
In hearts intertwined, they nurture the flame,
Through trials and joys, they honor His name.

Blessed are the gentle, who offer their hand,
In kindness and love, together they stand.
Their laughter, a hymn that dances on air,
In the beatitudes, they flourish with care.

Blessed are the seekers of truth and of grace,
With open hearts, in each sacred space.
Together they journey through shadows and light,
In the embrace of love, they ignite the night.

Blessed are the souls who share in the feast,
From struggling hearts, He brings forth the least.
In sharing their burdens, they blossom as one,
In the beatitudes, their hope shines like sun.

Blessed are the faithful, who dance in the rain,
In joy and in sorrow, they'll never wane.
United in spirit, their love only grows,
In the beatitudes of togetherness, it shows.

When Love Becomes Our Refuge

When storms rage around us, love stands tall,
A steady fortress, it shelters us all.
In quiet moments, we find our peace,
When love is our refuge, our fears release.

In the depths of despair, a soft whisper calls,
A beacon of hope as the darkness falls.
With arms wide open, it beckons us near,
A sanctuary found, where voids disappear.

With every heartbeat, love whispers of grace,
In trials endured, we find our place.
Together we gather, in faith we unite,
When love becomes refuge, hearts shine so bright.

In laughter and tears, we draw ever close,
Embraced by the love that we cherish the most.
When shadows encroach, we look up above,
In the warmth of our refuge, we call it love.

Through valleys we tread, love lights up the way,
A guide for our journey, a dawn of new day.
When love is our refuge, our spirits ignite,
We walk ever forward, embraced by the light.

A Communion of Souls in Light

In the sacred silence, two hearts align,
A communion of souls, in love they entwine.
With prayerful whispers, their spirits ascend,
In the presence of light, where earthly ties mend.

Through each gentle touch, they feel the divine,
In moments of grace, their souls intertwine.
With laughter and tears, they journey as one,
In the dance of the spirit, their fears come undone.

In unity found, their hearts beat as one,
Together they walk, beneath the same sun.
Where love knows no bounds, and mercy flows free,
In a communion of souls, they find harmony.

With every shared glance, a story unfolds,
Of triumph and trials, of dreams yet untold.
In the tapestry woven, they glimpse the divine,
In a communion of souls, their spirits align.

In light and in love, their visions expand,
As they lift up each other, together they stand.
In this sacred embrace, forever they'll be,
In a communion of souls, where love is the key.

Embraced by the Divine

In the silence we find grace,
Whispers of love in sacred space.
Hands raised high, hearts intertwined,
In each moment, His light defined.

Through trials and joy, we learn to see,
The gentle touch of the holy decree.
Guided by faith, we walk as one,
In the warmth of the Holy Son.

With every breath, our spirits rise,
Transcending earth, we seek the skies.
In the embrace of the Divine,
We lose ourselves, our souls align.

Together we sing, a melody bright,
United in trust, we shine with light.
Through the storm, our love remains,
In His arms, all fear wanes.

In shadows deep, we find our path,
A journey blessed with love's sweet math.
With open hearts, we linger near,
In every moment, the Divine is clear.

Embraced by grace, we rise above,
In this circle, we share our love.
With faith as our guide, we find the way,
Together in spirit, we choose to stay.

Starlit Promises

In the night, the stars do shine,
Each one a promise, a truth divine.
Whispers of hope in the cosmic dance,
Inviting us all to take a chance.

With every twinkle, every glow,
A reminder of love, a gentle flow.
Dreams alight on starlit beams,
Guiding our hearts through boundless dreams.

In the stillness, we find our way,
By the light of those guiding rays.
Each flicker a prayer, a voice of grace,
An echo of love in the vastness of space.

Hold fast to dreams under the night,
In unity, we find our might.
Together we shine, a brilliant hue,
Starlit promises, forever true.

As the cosmos sings its song of life,
We rise above the worldly strife.
With hope in our hearts, we share the light,
In the tapestry of love, everything's right.

So lift your gaze, let your spirit soar,
In the beauty of night, we're never unsure.
With starlit promises, we find our way,
In the embrace of the night, forever we'll stay.

Journey of the Beloved

On the path where love is found,
In every heartbeat, a sacred sound.
Journeying together, hand in hand,
With every step, we understand.

Through valleys low and mountains high,
In each other's eyes, we touch the sky.
Bound by love, our souls entwined,
In every challenge, grace we find.

With every whisper, we speak the truth,
In the innocence and joy of youth.
The road may twist, but we'll not stray,
For love's compass will show the way.

In the tapestry of life we weave,
With threads of faith, we choose to believe.
In every moment, our spirits sing,
In the warmth of love, we find our wings.

As stars align above us bright,
A testament to love's pure light.
Through every trial and every tear,
Together we rise, casting out fear.

So let us walk, the journey unfolds,
In the arms of love, our story told.
With hearts ablaze, forever bold,
In the journey of the beloved, love is gold.

A Prayer for Togetherness

In the stillness, we raise our hands,
A prayer of hope across the lands.
Let every heart feel love's embrace,
In unity, we find our place.

For every sorrow and every joy,
Together we stand, no fear can destroy.
In the bond of faith, we find our way,
Let love guide us, come what may.

As the world around us starts to change,
In kindness and grace, we rearrange.
With open hearts, we gather near,
In the power of love, we conquer fear.

In moments shared, our spirits soar,
With each whispered prayer, we seek for more.
Let love be the light that shines so bright,
In the heart of darkness, our guiding light.

Together we rise, a collective song,
In harmony, where we belong.
With love as our anchor, we shall stand,
In a world united, hand in hand.

So let us pray for bonds so true,
In every heart, let love break through.
For in togetherness, we find our peace,
A prayer for love that will never cease.

In Reverence of Our Journey

With every step upon this road,
We carry faith as our true load.
The path is lit by love's pure light,
Guiding us through the darkest night.

As we walk hand in hand, side by side,
In grace and mercy, our hearts abide.
Every trial shapes our souls anew,
In reverence, we honor what's true.

The sacred moments bring us near,
In whispers soft, we share our fear.
But united, we rise above,
Transcending all through endless love.

Each dawn reveals a brand new chance,
To dance with hope in faith's sweet dance.
Together we weave our story bright,
Illuminated by heaven's light.

Through valleys deep and mountains high,
Our spirits soar as we touch the sky.
In reverence, our hearts now sing,
Of the boundless joy true love can bring.

The Sanctuary of Our Joined Hearts

Within our hearts, a sacred space,
A refuge born of love's embrace.
In silence shared, we hear the call,
For in this bond, we shall not fall.

Each prayer we whisper, each tear we shed,
Builds the sanctuary where we are led.
With hope entwined in every breath,
We celebrate life, defying death.

In trust renewed, our spirits blend,
A testament that love won't end.
Together, we seek divine design,
In shadows cast, we brightly shine.

With every heartbeat, we are made whole,
In the sanctuary of the soul.
United in purpose, we shall soar,
Grateful for love and forevermore.

Let our joined hearts echo the grace,
Of gentle smiles and warm embrace.
In the sacredness of this part,
We find the light of a loving heart.

Wings of Faith Beneath the Stars

Beneath the stars, our dreams take flight,
On wings of faith, we chase the light.
With open hearts, we dare to seek,
The path that makes our spirits speak.

Each twinkling star, a promise made,
In the tapestry of love displayed.
Guided by hope, we journey far,
Finding solace where blessings are.

In the quiet night, we hear the voice,
Of heavenly whispers that help us rejoice.
With each guiding star, our fears release,
In the embrace of faith, we find our peace.

Together we rise on faith's embrace,
In the vast expanse, we find our place.
With every breath, we rise and ascend,
On wings of love that never end.

So when doubt clouds our yearning sight,
We lift our gaze to the gentle night.
With wings of faith beneath the stars,
We trust the journey, despite the scars.

Love as a Steadfast Lighthouse

In stormy seas, when shadows creep,
Love stands firm, a promise to keep.
Like a lighthouse shining so bright,
Guiding us home through the darkest night.

Its beacon calls to our weary hearts,
A flame that glows and never departs.
With every wave that crashes down,
Love remains our solid ground.

When storms may rage and hope seems lost,
We cling to love, accepting the cost.
In embrace, we find courage anew,
Love, our compass, forever true.

Through trials faced and battles fought,
In love's embrace, we find what's sought.
A steadfast light, forever it shines,
Illuminating the sacred signs.

So let our hearts be vessels of grace,
Reflecting love in this vast space.
As long as there are storms to fight,
Love will be our steadfast light.

Tapestry of Our Togetherness

In the fabric of love so fine,
Threads of kindness intertwine,
Each heart a stitch, each soul a beam,
Together we weave, we share a dream.

In laughter and tears, we find our place,
Embracing each other with gentle grace,
In moments of silence, our spirits dance,
Bound by the love of a sacred chance.

Through trials and joys, we walk as one,
With faith as our guide, we rise with the sun,
In unity strong, our voices align,
A tapestry bright, forever divine.

Hand in hand, we stand so tall,
Lifting each other, we answer the call,
In the warmth of prayer, our hopes combine,
A beautiful story, forever entwined.

Together we journey, our hearts ablaze,
In the light of His love, we sing His praise,
Each moment a thread, a sacred embrace,
In the tapestry of faith, we find our place.

The Altar of Connection

At the altar of hearts, we come to kneel,
In the quiet whispers, our spirits heal,
With every prayer offered, we lay down fears,
In the bond of connection, we dry our tears.

In the circle of trust, we gather near,
Each voice a blessing, each soul sincere,
Through shared revelations, our faith takes flight,
Together we stand, embracing the light.

The warmth of community, a sacred flame,
Igniting our purpose, in love's sweet name,
In the echo of laughter, we find our song,
In the rhythm of grace, where we all belong.

With open arms, we share our plight,
Finding strength in numbers, igniting the night,
In every connection, a promise we make,
To cherish each other, for love's own sake.

In the tapestry woven, our lives align,
At the altar of connection, our spirits entwine,
Through journeys unknown, we walk hand in hand,
In the beauty of faith, forever we stand.

A Legacy of Faithful Hearts

A legacy built on love's gentle way,
In the harvest of hope, we gather and pray,
With seeds of compassion, we plant in the ground,
A garden of faith, where blessings abound.

With every generation, our stories unite,
A tapestry rich, with colors so bright,
In the echoes of elders, wisdom we find,
A faithful commitment, through heart and mind.

Through trials and triumphs, we honor the past,
In the shadows of doubt, our love holds fast,
With hands raised in gratitude, we sing our part,
A legacy woven from faithful hearts.

In unity's journey, we forge the way,
With love as our compass, we'll never sway,
Together we journey, through joy and strife,
Creating a legacy that breathes with life.

In the warmth of remembrance, we gather once more,
Celebrating the blessings we've come to adore,
In the flames of affection, our spirits ignite,
A legacy of faithful hearts, shining bright.

Prayers Woven into Time

In the fabric of time, our prayers arise,
Whispers of hope that reach to the skies,
Each moment a thread, with purpose and grace,
Together we weave, in this sacred space.

Through seasons of sorrow, through joy's embrace,
Our prayers are the stitches that hold each place,
In the quiet of night, in the glow of the dawn,
We gather our thoughts, together we're drawn.

With every prayer spoken, our souls intertwine,
In the harmony found, our spirits align,
With faith as our anchor, love as our guide,
In the tapestry of time, together we bide.

As rivers of prayer flow endlessly wide,
We find in each other our hearts open wide,
In the journey of faith, through each twist and turn,
The fires of devotion, eternally burn.

For in the weaving of prayers so true,
We find the connection that dwells within you,
In the beauty of stillness, in the song of our rhyme,
We cherish each moment, our prayers woven into time.

The Tree of Shared Blessings

In the garden where spirits meet,
Roots entwined, our hearts do greet.
Leaves whisper secrets from above,
Branching out in sacred love.

Fruits of kindness, grown with care,
Nurtured by the prayers we share.
Together in this holy space,
Finding joy in every trace.

Seasons change, yet we remain,
In the light, beyond the pain.
Beneath the tree, our voices rise,
Praising blessings from the skies.

With gentle storms, our faith is tested,
Yet still in joy, our souls are rested.
Through darker nights, we seek the dawn,
Our bond, like roots, forever drawn.

In unity, we stand so tall,
Answering the loving call.
The tree of blessings, strong and true,
A haven for me and you.

The Embrace of Transcendent Love

In the stillness of the night,
Hearts entwined, we find our light.
A love that transcends time and space,
Wraps us in a warm embrace.

Every tear, a sacred stream,
Flowing softly, like a dream.
In each moment, grace does bloom,
Illuminating every room.

Together, we dance in the divine,
Trusting whispers, yours and mine.
In every heartbeat, love's sweet song,
Guides us gently, where we belong.

As the stars kiss the velvet sky,
We rise above, we soar, we fly.
Hand in hand, we do our part,
Echoing faith within the heart.

In this bond, the world is whole,
Two souls intertwined, one goal.
Transcendent love, forever free,
In unity, eternally.

In the Fabric of the Divine

Woven threads of sacred grace,
Craft our lives in this vast space.
In every stitch, a tale is told,
Of love and faith, brave and bold.

Patterns bloom in vibrant hues,
Guided by the light we choose.
Each moment, a tapestry spun,
Intertwining, two become one.

In silence, we hear the call,
A sacred pulse connecting all.
The fabric stretches, breathes and sighs,
Reflecting truth before our eyes.

Through trials, seams may fray and wear,
But love restores with tender care.
In the tapestry, we find our place,
An endless dance of warm embrace.

Each thread, a prayer softly spoken,
In this grand design, love is unbroken.
The fabric of the divine we weave,
Inviting all to love and believe.

Kisses of Light in the Shadows

In twilight's hush, a whisper calls,
A dance of shadows, softly falls.
Yet in the dark, a spark ignites,
Kisses of light, the heart excites.

Through trials faced, we learn to see,
Illumination sets us free.
In every struggle, hope shines bright,
Guiding us through the endless night.

With every tear, a beam of grace,
Shadows tremble in love's embrace.
In quiet corners, whispers bloom,
Transforming fear into sweet room.

The dawn arrives, releasing fears,
Kisses of light dry all our tears.
Heaven's promise, always near,
Comfort found in love's sweet cheer.

We are the stars that light the way,
In the darkest night, we find our sway.
Kisses of light, forever show,
In each shadow, love will grow.

The Covenant of Heartstrings

In whispers soft, our promise made,
Two souls entwined, though shadows fade.
A bond unbroken, a sacred thread,
In light of love, our spirits fed.

Through trials faced, we stand as one,
In laughter shared, and battles won.
For in your eyes, the truth I find,
A journey shared, two hearts aligned.

With every tear and joy we share,
A tapestry woven with tender care.
In faith we trust, and grace we seek,
Our hearts united, no need to speak.

Together we rise, through storm and strife,
A testament to this sacred life.
In the embrace of love's sweet song,
Together we journey, where we belong.

The covenant strong, forever we vow,
In moments fleeting, we cherish now.
With every breath, our spirits soar,
In love's embrace, forevermore.

Celestial Ties in the Night

Under starlit skies, we find our grace,
In the quiet hush, we seek your face.
With every twinkle, a prayer we weave,
In this sacred space, we believe.

The moonlight dances on the sea,
A melody sweet, our hearts agree.
Each whisper shared in the still of night,
In love's embrace, we find our light.

The heavens open, blessings rain,
A bond unyielding, through joy and pain.
In every heartbeat, a sacred tie,
Together we rise, like eagles high.

In moments of silence, our spirits cling,
To the songs of hope that love can bring.
With every star, a promise anew,
Together we shine, forever true.

So let the night wrap us in its glow,
In celestial ties, our spirits grow.
In faith, we trust, our hearts ignite,
In the beauty of love, our souls take flight.

Blessings of Our Togetherness

In the warmth of dawn, our spirits meet,
With gratitude deep, our hearts beat.
For every blessing, a gift we share,
In the dance of life, we find our care.

Through every trial, your hand in mine,
A sacred journey, oh how divine.
With laughter bright and tears that flow,
In this togetherness, our love will grow.

We gather strength in unity's bond,
In moments cherished, of which we're fond.
With every sunrise, a chance anew,
In blessings showered, I see us through.

Together we weave a tapestry bright,
In the fabric of love, we find our light.
With faith unshaken, our spirits sing,
In the joy of togetherness, love's offering.

So let us savor each moment we share,
In the garden of life, we nurture with care.
For in our embrace, the world falls away,
In blessings of love, forever we stay.

Pillars of Enduring Faith

In the shadows cast by trials faced,
Stand we together, our spirits graced.
With each prayer whispered, a promise made,
In the pillars of faith, we are not afraid.

Through storms that rage and winds that blow,
In the strength of love, we find our flow.
With steadfast hearts, we face the night,
In hope's embrace, we gather light.

The foundations built on trust remain,
In every moment, through joy and pain.
With courage bold, our spirits soar,
In the pillars of faith, we seek for more.

Together we stand, unyielding, strong,
In love so pure, where we belong.
For in each heartbeat lies the grace,
Of enduring faith, our sacred space.

So let us rise with hearts alight,
In the journey shared, we face the night.
With every step, our spirits embraced,
In the pillars of faith, we find our place.

Echoes of Faithful Togetherness

In the stillness of the night, we pray,
Whispers rise, guiding our way.
Heartbeats sync in unseen grace,
Together, we seek a sacred space.

In the light of dawn, hope shines,
Hands joined, we draw the lines.
Each smile a spark, each tear a plea,
Bound by faith, forever we're free.

Through trials, we stand side by side,
In love's embrace, we shall abide.
Voices lift in joyous song,
A chorus sweet that carries us along.

Let the world fade, it matters not,
For in our hearts, love is sought.
Together we tread this sacred ground,
In echoes of faith, true peace is found.

As stars align in the night sky,
United in spirit, we soar high.
With every step, we pave the way,
In faithful togetherness, come what may.

Threads of Existence Woven in Love

In every thread, a story spun,
Life's great tapestry begun.
With gentle hands, we craft and bind,
Each heart a treasure, lovingly aligned.

Through trials faced and joys embraced,
Every moment, we are graced.
In laughter shared, in tears we weep,
Our souls entwined, forever deep.

In the fabric of existence, we find
The ties that bind, the love that's kind.
With every stitch, we weave our fate,
Threads of existence, love's true state.

With kindness, we cloak those in need,
In love's great garden, we must plant the seed.
Through unity, we shall endure,
In the warmth of love, our hearts are pure.

As dusk gives way to dawn's embrace,
We gather strength, together we face.
In life's grand weave, forever we stand,
Each thread a blessing, hand in hand.

The Harmonious Accord of Being

In harmony's tune, we find our song,
In the sacred dance, we all belong.
Every note a promise, every beat a prayer,
Together we rise, our spirits laid bare.

In unity's embrace, hearts align,
Whispers of love in every sign.
Each moment shared, a gift divine,
In the harmonious accord, our souls intertwine.

With hands uplifted, we give our praise,
For the light that guides through all our days.
In laughter and silence, we weave our fate,
In the dance of being, we celebrate.

Through valleys low and mountains high,
In each other's presence, we learn to fly.
Together we weather the storms that pass,
In the harmonious accord, our spirits mass.

Let love be the music that fills the air,
In every breath, we show we care.
In the tapestry of existence, we find the key,
In the harmonious accord, we are truly free.

Celestial Dances of Devotion

In the cosmos vast, we twirl and spin,
To the rhythm of faith, we let love in.
Stars align in celestial grace,
In every glance, a holy embrace.

With every heartbeat, the universe sings,
In devotion's dance, our spirit takes wings.
In the warmth of the sun, in the cool of the night,
We gather together, hearts burning bright.

Through time's great flow, we journey as one,
In the celestial dance, our prayers are spun.
Each twinkle a blessing, each comet a sign,
In the cosmic ballet, our souls entwined.

With gratitude rising, we soar so high,
In devotion's embrace, we touch the sky.
Through ages and seasons, forever we'll sway,
In celestial dances, we find our way.

Let love be our compass, forever we roam,
In the dance of devotion, we find our home.
With every move, we honor, we bless,
In the celestial night, we are truly possessed.

Sacred Threads of Connection

In quiet corners where hearts reside,
We weave our hopes with love as our guide.
Threads of faith bind us, oh so tight,
In the sacred dance of day and night.

Beneath the heavens, where whispers speak,
Together we gather, the strong and the weak.
In shared devotion, we find our way,
As the spirit's light begins to play.

A tapestry woven with prayers and dreams,
Every heartbeat echoes, or so it seems.
In the arms of grace, our souls convene,
Embracing the mystery, a love unseen.

The bonds of kindness, like stars align,
On the sacred path, our souls entwine.
In stillness we find the wisdom we seek,
Guided by whispers, gentle and meek.

Together we rise, in unity strong,
Singing the verses of the ages long.
In the sacred threads, our spirits soar,
Connected in love, forevermore.

Faith's Embrace

Within the shelter of faith we stand,
Holding each other, hand in hand.
Every prayer a promise, softly sung,
In the heart's quiet chamber, love is spun.

In the evening glow, shadows may dance,
But faith's embrace gives us a chance.
To rise above the trials that bind,
In the arms of grace, true peace we find.

With every heartbeat, a sacred vow,
To trust in the light that guides us now.
In the smile of a stranger, we see the face,
Of the divine, a warm embrace.

Through storms we wander, yet never alone,
In the depths of our spirits, love has grown.
Faith is the anchor, sturdy and bright,
Guiding our souls through the darkest night.

We gather together, a circle of light,
With open hearts, prepared for the fight.
In the coded whispers of love's sweet song,
In faith's embrace, forever we belong.

Tethered Spirits Divine

In the vast expanse where stars collide,
Our spirits tethered, side by side.
In the sacred dance, we find our way,
Guided by faith and love's soft sway.

Through valleys low and mountains high,
Our connection glimmers like the dawn sky.
With each gentle breeze that brushes past,
We feel the presence of the divine cast.

In moments quiet, when silence speaks,
The whispers of grace fill all that seeks.
In every heartbeat, a thread is spun,
Binding our souls till our days are done.

With joy we gather, in spirit and truth,
Renewing our vows, embracing our youth.
In laughter shared, in sorrows that blend,
The tethered spirits, forever friends.

As the journey unfolds, in light we walk,
In circles of peace, where love can talk.
Tethered to hope, in a world divine,
Together we shine, as stars align.

In the Light of Unity

In the light of unity, we rise as one,
Bound by the love that cannot be undone.
Each heart a beacon, shining so bright,
Guiding us gently through the darkest night.

With open arms, we welcome the grace,
In every encounter, the sacred space.
Our voices blend in a harmonious song,
In the dance of the spirit, we all belong.

Together we journey, hand in hand,
In the warmth of love, together we stand.
Each shared story, a thread we weave,
In the light of unity, we shall believe.

As we walk the path, embracing the light,
In the depths of our souls, a shimmering sight.
With every step, we journey as one,
In the light of unity, our hearts have spun.

With gratitude flowing like rivers wide,
In the circle of love, we shall abide.
In the light of unity, the truth is clear,
Connected forever, with love sincere.

Milton Keynes UK
Ingram Content Group UK Ltd.
UKHW022118251124
451529UK00012B/591

9 789916 897942